MAD LIBS®

GRAB BAG MAD LIBS

By Roger Price and Leonard St

PSS!
PRICE STERN SLOAN

PRICE STERN SLOAN
Published by the Penguin Group
Penguin Group (USA) Inc., 375 Hudson Street, New York, New York 10014, USA
Penguin Group (Canada), 90 Eglinton Avenue East, Suite 700,
Toronto, Ontario M4P 2Y3, Canada
(a division of Pearson Penguin Canada Inc.)
Penguin Books Ltd., 80 Strand, London WC2R 0RL, England
Penguin Group Ireland, 25 St. Stephen's Green, Dublin 2, Ireland
(a division of Penguin Books Ltd.)
Penguin Group (Australia), 250 Camberwell Road, Camberwell,
Victoria 3124, Australia
(a division of Pearson Australia Group Pty. Ltd.)
Penguin Books India Pvt. Ltd., 11 Community Centre, Panchsheel Park,
New Delhi—110 017, India
Penguin Group (NZ), 67 Apollo Drive, Rosedale, North Shore 0632, New Zealand
(a division of Pearson New Zealand Ltd.)
Penguin Books (South Africa) (Pty.) Ltd., 24 Sturdee Avenue,
Rosebank, Johannesburg 2196, South Africa

Penguin Books Ltd., Registered Offices: 80 Strand, London WC2R 0RL, England

Published by Price Stern Sloan,
a division of Penguin Young Readers Group,
345 Hudson Street, New York, New York 10014.

ISBN 978-0-8431-3894-8

15 17 19 20 18 16

MAD LIBS®
INSTRUCTIONS

MAD LIBS® is a game for people who don't like games!
It can be played by one, two, three, four, or forty.

• RIDICULOUSLY SIMPLE DIRECTIONS

In this tablet you will find stories containing blank spaces where words are left out. One player, the READER, selects one of these stories. The READER does not tell anyone what the story is about. Instead, he/she asks the other players, the WRITERS, to give him/her words. These words are used to fill in the blank spaces in the story.

• TO PLAY

The READER asks each WRITER in turn to call out a word—an adjective or a noun or whatever the space calls for—and uses them to fill in the blank spaces in the story. The result is a MAD LIBS® game.

When the READER then reads the completed MAD LIBS® game to the other players, they will discover that they have written a story that is fantastic, screamingly funny, shocking, silly, crazy, or just plain dumb—depending upon which words each WRITER called out.

• EXAMPLE (*Before* and *After*)

" _____ !" he said _____
      EXCLAMATION   ADVERB

as he jumped into his convertible _____ and
                                        NOUN

drove off with his _____ wife.
                        ADJECTIVE

" *Ouch!* !" he said *stupidly*
      EXCLAMATION   ADVERB

as he jumped into his convertible *cat* and
                                          NOUN

drove off with his *brave* wife.
                        ADJECTIVE

In case you have forgotten what adjectives, adverbs, nouns, and verbs are, here is a quick review:

An ADJECTIVE describes something or somebody. *Lumpy, soft, ugly, messy,* and *short* are adjectives.

An ADVERB tells how something is done. It modifies a verb and usually ends in "ly." *Modestly, stupidly, greedily,* and *carefully* are adverbs.

A NOUN is the name of a person, place or thing. *Sidewalk, umbrella, bridle, bathtub,* and *nose* are nouns.

A VERB is an action word. *Run, pitch, jump,* and *swim* are verbs. Put the verbs in past tense if the directions say PAST TENSE. *Ran, pitched, jumped,* and *swam* are verbs in the past tense.

When we ask for a PLACE, we mean any sort of place: a country or city *(Spain, Cleveland)* or a room *(bathroom, kitchen.)*

An EXCLAMATION or SILLY WORD is any sort of funny sound, gasp, grunt, or outcry, like *Wow!, Ouch!, Whomp!, Ick!,* and *Gadzooks!*

When we ask for specific words, like a NUMBER, a COLOR, an ANIMAL, or a PART OF THE BODY, we mean a word that is one of those things, like *seven, blue, horse,* or *head.*

When we ask for a PLURAL, it means more than one. For example, *cat* pluralized is *cats.*

MAD LIBS® is fun to play with friends, but you can also play it by yourself! To begin with, DO NOT look at the story on the page below. Fill in the blanks on this page with the words called for. Then, using the words you have selected, fill in the blank spaces in the story.

Now you've created your own hilarious MAD LIBS® game!

INTERVIEW WITH A ROCK STAR

PLURAL NOUN _____

PLURAL NOUN _____

NOUN _____

COLOR _____

VERB _____

ADJECTIVE _____

NOUN _____

NOUN _____

ADJECTIVE _____

ADJECTIVE _____

NUMBER _____

ADJECTIVE _____

ADJECTIVE _____

ADJECTIVE _____

NOUN _____

VERB _____

MAD LIBS
INTERVIEW WITH A ROCK STAR

QUESTION: Whatever made you choose the name "The Psycho

_____ " for your group?
   PLURAL NOUN

ANSWER: All the other good names like the "Rolling _____,"
                                                  PLURAL NOUN

"_____ Jam," and "_____ Floyd" were taken.
      NOUN   COLOR

QUESTION: You not only _____ songs, but you play
                              VERB

many _____ instruments, don't you?
         ADJECTIVE

ANSWER: Yes. I play the electric _____, the bass
                                          NOUN

_____ , and the _____ keyboard.
      NOUN   ADJECTIVE

QUESTION: You now have a/an _____ song that is
                                   ADJECTIVE

number _____ on the _____ charts. What was
         NUMBER   ADJECTIVE

the inspiration for this _____ song?
                              ADJECTIVE

ANSWER: Believe it or not, it was a/an _____ song that
                                             ADJECTIVE

my mother used to sing to me when it was time for _____,
                                                        NOUN

and it never failed to _____ me to sleep.
                            VERB

From GRAB BAG MAD LIBS® • Copyright © 2001, 1996 by Price Stern Sloan,
a division of Penguin Putnam Books for Young Readers, New York.

MAD LIBS® is fun to play with friends, but you can also play it by yourself! To begin with, DO NOT look at the story on the page below. Fill in the blanks on this page with the words called for. Then, using the words you have selected, fill in the blank spaces in the story.

Now you've created your own hilarious MAD LIBS® game!

HAVE I GOT A GIRAFFE FOR YOU!

PLURAL NOUN _____

PLURAL NOUN _____

PART OF THE BODY _____

NUMBER _____

PLURAL NOUN _____

PART OF THE BODY _____

TYPE OF LIQUID _____

PART OF THE BODY (PLURAL) _____

PART OF THE BODY _____

ADJECTIVE_____

PLURAL NOUN _____

ADJECTIVE_____

ADJECTIVE_____

VERB ENDING IN "ING" _____

NOUN _____

PLURAL NOUN _____

NOUN _____

MAD LIBS®
HAVE I GOT
A GIRAFFE FOR YOU!

Giraffes have aroused the curiosity of _____ since earliest
PLURAL NOUN

times. The giraffe is the tallest of all living _____ , but
PLURAL NOUN

scientists are unable to explain how it got its long _____ .
PART OF THE BODY

The giraffe's tremendous height, which might reach _____
NUMBER

_____ , comes mostly from its legs and _____ .
PLURAL NOUN   PART OF THE BODY

If a giraffe wants to take a drink of _____ from the ground, it
TYPE OF LIQUID

has to spread its _____ far apart in order to reach
PART OF THE BODY (PLURAL)

down and lap up the water with its huge _____ . The
PART OF THE BODY

giraffe has _____ ears that are sensitive to the faintest
ADJECTIVE

_____ , and it has a/an _____ sense of smell
PLURAL NOUN   ADJECTIVE

and sight. When attacked, a giraffe can put up a/an _____
ADJECTIVE

fight by _____ out with its hind legs and using its
VERB ENDING IN "ING"

head like a sledge _____ . Finally, a giraffe can gallop at
NOUN

more than thirty _____ an hour when pursued and can
PLURAL NOUN

outrun the fastest _____ .
NOUN

MAD LIBS® is fun to play with friends, but you can also play it by yourself! To begin with, DO NOT look at the story on the page below. Fill in the blanks on this page with the words called for. Then, using the words you have selected, fill in the blank spaces in the story.

Now you've created your own hilarious MAD LIBS® game!

THE OLYMPICS

NOUN _____

PLURAL NOUN _____

ADJECTIVE_____

PLURAL NOUN _____

PLURAL NOUN _____

NUMBER _____

ADJECTIVE_____

ADJECTIVE_____

NOUN _____

ADJECTIVE_____

VERB ENDING IN "S"_____

PART OF THE BODY _____

NOUN _____

ADJECTIVE_____

PLURAL NOUN _____

PLURAL NOUN _____

MAD LIBS®
THE OLYMPICS

Every four years, countries from all over the _____ send
NOUN

their best _____ to compete in _____
PLURAL NOUN   ADJECTIVE

games and win _____. These events are called the
PLURAL NOUN

Olympic _____, and they started _____ years ago
PLURAL NOUN   NUMBER

in _____ Greece. When a winner receives his or her
ADJECTIVE

_____ medal at the games, the national _____
ADJECTIVE   NOUN

of his or her country is played by a/an _____ band.
ADJECTIVE

As the band _____, the citizens of that country put
VERB ENDING IN "S"

their _____ to their chest and join in the singing of
PART OF THE BODY

their national _____. Thanks to television, these
NOUN

_____ events can now be watched by over a billion
ADJECTIVE

_____ throughout the world every four _____.
PLURAL NOUN   PLURAL NOUN

From GRAB BAG MAD LIBS® • Copyright © 2001, 1996 by Price Stern Sloan,
a division of Penguin Putnam Books for Young Readers, New York.

MAD LIBS® is fun to play with friends, but you can also play it by yourself! To begin with, DO NOT look at the story on the page below. Fill in the blanks on this page with the words called for. Then, using the words you have selected, fill in the blank spaces in the story.

Now you've created your own hilarious MAD LIBS® game!

HOME SWEET HOME

NOUN _____

PART OF THE BODY _____

NUMBER _____

NOUN _____

COLOR _____

ADJECTIVE _____

NOUN _____

NOUN _____

PLURAL NOUN _____

NOUN _____

NOUN _____

ADJECTIVE _____

NOUN _____

ADVERB _____

PART OF THE BODY _____

VERB ENDING IN "ING" _____

ADJECTIVE _____

MAD LIBS®
HOME SWEET HOME

Some people are fond of the saying, "Home is where you hang your

_____ ." Others say, "Home is where the _____
NOUN   PART OF THE BODY

is." As for me, even though my home is a rustic, _____ -story
                                                  NUMBER

_____ home with a/an _____ picket fence
NOUN   COLOR

surrounding it, I think of it as my _____ castle. Perched
                                     ADJECTIVE

on a/an _____ overlooking a babbling _____
          NOUN   NOUN

and surrounded by a forest of huge _____ , my home offers
                                     PLURAL NOUN

me _____ and tranquility. Each and every _____
     NOUN   NOUN

I look forward to coming back to my _____ home, where
                                     ADJECTIVE

my faithful _____ will _____ greet me
             NOUN   ADVERB

by wagging its _____ and _____ all over
                PART OF THE BODY   VERB ENDING IN "ING"

me. I just love my home _____ home.
                          ADJECTIVE

From GRAB BAG MAD LIBS® • Copyright © 2001, 1996 by Price Stern Sloan,
a division of Penguin Putnam Books for Young Readers, New York.

MAD LIBS® is fun to play with friends, but you can also play it by yourself! To begin with, DO NOT look at the story on the page below. Fill in the blanks on this page with the words called for. Then, using the words you have selected, fill in the blank spaces in the story.

Now you've created your own hilarious MAD LIBS® game!

INTERVIEW WITH A COMEDIAN

NOUN _____

ADJECTIVE _____

ADJECTIVE _____

NOUN _____

NUMBER _____

PLURAL NOUN _____

NOUN _____

VERB _____

VERB _____

PLURAL NOUN _____

PLURAL NOUN _____

ADJECTIVE _____

NOUN _____

MAD☺LIBS®
INTERVIEW WITH
A COMEDIAN

QUESTION: Were you always a stand-up _____?

NOUN

ANSWER: No. I had many _____ jobs in my _____

ADJECTIVE   ADJECTIVE

lifetime. I started out as a used _____ salesperson, and

NOUN

then for _____ years, I sold ladies' _____ .

NUMBER   PLURAL NOUN

QUESTION: When did you discover you were a funny _____

NOUN

who could make people _____ out loud?

VERB

ANSWER: It was in school. The first time our teacher had us do show

and _____ , I made the _____ in my class

VERB   PLURAL NOUN

laugh so hard they fell out of their _____ .

PLURAL NOUN

QUESTION: How would you describe your _____ act?

ADJECTIVE

ANSWER: I am a thinking person's _____ .

NOUN

MAD LIBS® is fun to play with friends, but you can also play it by yourself! To begin with, DO NOT look at the story on the page below. Fill in the blanks on this page with the words called for. Then, using the words you have selected, fill in the blank spaces in the story.

Now you've created your own hilarious MAD LIBS® game!

MOVIES SHOULD BE FUN

PLURAL NOUN _____

ADJECTIVE _____

PLURAL NOUN _____

NOUN _____

ADJECTIVE _____

NOUN _____

NOUN _____

PERSON IN ROOM (MALE) _____

PLACE _____

ADJECTIVE _____

ANOTHER PERSON IN ROOM _____

ANOTHER PERSON IN ROOM _____

ADJECTIVE _____

PLURAL NOUN _____

PART OF THE BODY (PLURAL) _____

MAD LIBS®
MOVIES SHOULD BE FUN

In recent years, there have been too many disaster movies in which

tall _____ catch on fire, _____ dinosaurs come
PLURAL NOUN   ADJECTIVE

to life, and huge _____ attack people in the ocean, making
PLURAL NOUN

you afraid to get out of your _____ in the morning. Movie
NOUN

fans ask why we can't have more _____ pictures like
ADJECTIVE

It's a Wonderful _____ , *Gone with the* _____ ,
NOUN   NOUN

or *Mr.* _____ *Goes to* _____ . These films
PERSON IN ROOM (MALE)   PLACE

made you feel _____ all over. These same fans also ask
ADJECTIVE

why we can't have more funny films with comedians such as Laurel

and _____ , and Abbott and _____ .
ANOTHER PERSON IN ROOM   ANOTHER PERSON IN ROOM

These _____ performers gave us great slapstick
ADJECTIVE

_____ that still makes our _____ ache
PLURAL NOUN   PART OF THE BODY (PLURAL)

from laughing.

MAD LIBS® is fun to play with friends, but you can also play it by yourself! To begin with, DO NOT look at the story on the page below. Fill in the blanks on this page with the words called for. Then, using the words you have selected, fill in the blank spaces in the story.

Now you've created your own hilarious MAD LIBS® game!

COOL IT

PLURAL NOUN _____

ADJECTIVE _____

NOUN _____

ADJECTIVE _____

NOUN _____

NOUN _____

NOUN _____

NOUN _____

ADJECTIVE _____

VERB ENDING IN "ING" _____

NOUN _____

ADJECTIVE _____

NOUN _____

VERB _____

THE ART SCENE

Today the _____ Gallery presents a series of
             PERSON IN ROOM (LAST NAME)

_____ landscape paintings and still-life _____
  ADJECTIVE   PLURAL NOUN

by the _____ artist, _____ . These
        ADJECTIVE   PERSON IN ROOM (FULL NAME)

beautiful _____ will be on exhibition for the next
              PLURAL NOUN

three _____ .
        PLURAL NOUN

MUSIC

Tonight marks the _____ debut of the all-_____
             ADJECTIVE   NOUN

choir of _____ great _____ voices. This
       NUMBER   VERB ENDING IN "ING"

_____ ensemble will present _____ renditions
  ADJECTIVE   ADJECTIVE

of such _____ children's songs as "Twinkle Twinkle
        ADJECTIVE

Little _____ " and "Old MacDonald Had a _____ ."
     NOUN   NOUN

MAD LIBS® is fun to play with friends, but you can also play it by yourself! To begin with, DO NOT look at the story on the page below. Fill in the blanks on this page with the words called for. Then, using the words you have selected, fill in the blank spaces in the story.

Now you've created your own hilarious MAD LIBS® game!

THE THREE MUSKETEERS

ADJECTIVE_____

PLURAL NOUN _____

ADJECTIVE_____

NOUN _____

ADJECTIVE_____

NOUN _____

NOUN _____

PLURAL NOUN _____

NOUN _____

PERSON IN ROOM _____

PLURAL NOUN _____

ADJECTIVE_____

NOUN _____

NOUN _____

PLURAL NOUN _____

NOUN _____

MAD LIBS®
THE THREE MUSKETEERS

There is no more rousing story in _____ literature than
ADJECTIVE

The Three _____. This _____ romance
PLURAL NOUN   ADJECTIVE

by the great French _____, Alexander Dumas, tells the
NOUN

story of D'Artagnan, a/an _____ young _____
ADJECTIVE   NOUN

who arrives in 17th-century Paris riding a/an _____ with
NOUN

only three _____ in his pocket. Determined to be in the
PLURAL NOUN

service of the _____ who rules all of France, he duels
NOUN

with Athos, Pathos, and _____, three of the king's
PERSON IN ROOM

best _____. Eventually, these swordsmen and D'Artagnan
PLURAL NOUN

save their _____ king from being overthrown and losing
ADJECTIVE

his _____. Over the years, *The Three Musketeers* has been
NOUN

made into a stage _____, two motion _____,
NOUN   PLURAL NOUN

and, most recently, into a Broadway _____.
NOUN

MAD LIBS® is fun to play with friends, but you can also play it by yourself! To begin with, DO NOT look at the story on the page below. Fill in the blanks on this page with the words called for. Then, using the words you have selected, fill in the blank spaces in the story.

Now you've created your own hilarious MAD LIBS® game!

SNOW WHITE

PLURAL NOUN _____

PLURAL NOUN _____

ADJECTIVE_____

PLURAL NOUN _____

ADJECTIVE_____

NOUN _____

NOUN _____

ADJECTIVE_____

ADJECTIVE_____

PLURAL NOUN _____

NOUN _____

COLOR_____

NOUN _____

PART OF THE BODY _____

ADVERB_____

MAD LIBS®
SNOW WHITE

One of the most popular fairy _____ of all time is *Snow*
PLURAL NOUN

White and the Seven _____. Snow White is a princess
PLURAL NOUN

whose _____ beauty threatens her stepmother, the queen,
ADJECTIVE

and her two step- _____, who are very _____.
PLURAL NOUN   ADJECTIVE

Snow White is forced to flee from the _____ in which
NOUN

she lives and hide in the nearby _____. Once there, she
NOUN

is discovered by _____ animals who guide her to the
ADJECTIVE

_____ cottage of the seven dwarfs. The dwarfs come home
ADJECTIVE

from digging in their mine and discover Snow White asleep in their

_____. The dwarfs take care of her until a prince, who has
PLURAL NOUN

traveled the four corners of the _____ in search of Snow
NOUN

_____, arrives and gives her a magical _____
COLOR   NOUN

on her _____, which miraculously brings her back to
PART OF THE BODY

life. Snow White and the prince live _____ ever after.
ADVERB

MAD LIBS® is fun to play with friends, but you can also play it by yourself! To begin with, DO NOT look at the story on the page below. Fill in the blanks on this page with the words called for. Then, using the words you have selected, fill in the blank spaces in the story.

Now you've created your own hilarious MAD LIBS® game!

MAGIC, ANYONE?

PLURAL NOUN _____

ADJECTIVE _____

ADJECTIVE _____

NOUN _____

NOUN _____

NOUN _____

NOUN _____

ADJECTIVE _____

PART OF THE BODY _____

PLURAL NOUN _____

ADJECTIVE _____

NOUN _____

ADJECTIVE _____

NOUN _____

PART OF THE BODY (PLURAL) _____

PART OF THE BODY _____

PLURAL NOUN _____

_____ of all ages enjoy watching _____

PLURAL NOUN   ADJECTIVE

magicians perform their _____ tricks. Every man,

ADJECTIVE

woman, and _____ loves to see a magician pull a/an

NOUN

_____ out of a hat, saw a live _____

NOUN   NOUN

in half, or make a huge _____ disappear into

NOUN

_____ air. Audiences love when magicians perform sleight

ADJECTIVE

of _____ with a deck of _____, a/an

PART OF THE BODY   PLURAL NOUN

_____ coin, or a silk _____. The greatest

ADJECTIVE   NOUN

of all magicians was the _____ Harry Houdini, who was

ADJECTIVE

able to escape from a locked _____ even though his

NOUN

_____ were tied behind his _____ and

PART OF THE BODY (PLURAL)   PART OF THE BODY

his feet were wrapped in iron _____.

PLURAL NOUN

MAD LIBS® is fun to play with friends, but you can also play it by yourself! To begin with, DO NOT look at the story on the page below. Fill in the blanks on this page with the words called for. Then, using the words you have selected, fill in the blank spaces in the story.

Now you've created your own hilarious MAD LIBS® game!

THE BIG GAME

PLURAL NOUN _____

PERSON IN ROOM _____

NOUN _____

PERSON IN ROOM (LAST NAME) _____

PLURAL NOUN _____

CITY _____

PLURAL NOUN _____

CITY _____

PLURAL NOUN _____

NOUN _____

ADJECTIVE _____

ADJECTIVE _____

NOUN _____

NOUN _____

NOUN _____

VERB _____

ADJECTIVE _____

MAD LIBS®
THE BIG GAME

To be read with great enthusiasm!

Hello there, sports _____! This is _____, talk-

PLURAL NOUN   PERSON IN ROOM

ing to you from the press _____ in _____

NOUN   PERSON IN ROOM (LAST NAME)

Stadium, where 57,000 cheering _____ have gathered

PLURAL NOUN

to watch the _____ _____ take on

CITY   PLURAL NOUN

the _____ _____. Even though the

CITY   PLURAL NOUN

_____ is shining, it's a/an _____ cold day with

NOUN   ADJECTIVE

the temperature in the _____ 20s. A strong _____

ADJECTIVE   NOUN

is blowing fiercely across the playing _____ that will

NOUN

definitely affect the passing _____. We'll be back for

NOUN

the opening _____-off after a few words from our

VERB

_____ sponsor.

ADJECTIVE

MAD LIBS® is fun to play with friends, but you can also play it by yourself! To begin with, DO NOT look at the story on the page below. Fill in the blanks on this page with the words called for. Then, using the words you have selected, fill in the blank spaces in the story.

Now you've created your own hilarious MAD LIBS® game!

THINGS TO DO
THIS WEEKEND

PERSON IN ROOM (LAST NAME) _____

ADJECTIVE _____

PLURAL NOUN _____

PLURAL NOUN _____

NOUN _____

ADJECTIVE _____

NOUN _____

ADVERB _____

NOUN _____

ADJECTIVE _____

PLURAL NOUN _____

PERSON IN ROOM _____

ADJECTIVE _____

NOUN _____

ADJECTIVE _____

ADJECTIVE _____

NOUN _____

NOUN _____

ADJECTIVE _____

MAD LIBS®
THINGS TO DO
THIS WEEKEND

FILM

_____ Theaters offers a/an _____
PERSON IN ROOM (LAST NAME)   ADJECTIVE

program of foreign _____ never before seen in
                         PLURAL NOUN

American _____. The first film to be shown will be
            PLURAL NOUN

Henry and the _____. This is the _____
                    NOUN   ADJECTIVE

love story of a man and his _____. It will be shown
                                   NOUN

_____ until the end of the _____.
     ADVERB   NOUN

STAGE

Appearing in our _____ theater for the next three
                      ADJECTIVE

_____ is _____, that very
    PLURAL NOUN   PERSON IN ROOM

_____ star of stage, screen, and _____. He/she
     ADJECTIVE   NOUN

will be appearing with our _____ repertory company in
                                ADJECTIVE

nightly performances of William Shakespeare's _____
                                                       ADJECTIVE

comedy, *A Midsummer Night's* _____. Tickets can be
                                     NOUN

purchased now at the _____ office by telephone, fax,
                           NOUN

or _____ card.
        ADJECTIVE

From GRAB BAG MAD LIBS® • Copyright © 2001, 1996 by Price Stern Sloan,
a division of Penguin Putnam Books for Young Readers, New York.

MAD LIBS® is fun to play with friends, but you can also play it by yourself! To begin with, DO NOT look at the story on the page below. Fill in the blanks on this page with the words called for. Then, using the words you have selected, fill in the blank spaces in the story.

Now you've created your own hilarious MAD LIBS® game!

SCENE FROM A HORROR PICTURE

ADJECTIVE _____

PART OF THE BODY _____

PLURAL NOUN _____

NOUN _____

ADJECTIVE _____

PLURAL NOUN _____

EXCLAMATION _____

NOUN _____

PART OF THE BODY _____

PERSON IN ROOM _____

SUBJECT TAUGHT IN SCHOOL _____

NOUN _____

PART OF THE BODY _____

ADJECTIVE _____

VERB _____

ADVERB _____

NOUN _____

NOUN _____

MAD LIBS®
SCENE FROM A
HORROR PICTURE

To be read aloud (preferrably by live people):

Actor #1: Why did we have to come to this _____ old
ADJECTIVE

castle? This place sends shivers up and down my _____ .
PART OF THE BODY

Actor #2: We had no choice. You know all the _____ in
PLURAL NOUN

town were filled because of the _____ convention.
NOUN

Actor #1: I'd have been happy to stay in a/an _____ motel.
ADJECTIVE

Actor #2: Relax. Here comes the bellboy for our _____ .
PLURAL NOUN

Actor #1: _____ ! Look, he's all bent over and has a big
EXCLAMATION

_____ riding on his _____ . He looks just like
NOUN   PART OF THE BODY

_____ from that horror flick, *Frankenstein*.
PERSON IN ROOM

Actor #2: No. I think he's my old _____ teacher
SUBJECT TAUGHT IN SCHOOL

from _____ school.
NOUN

Actor #1: I'm putting my _____ down! I'm not staying in
PART OF THE BODY

this _____ place. I'd rather _____ in the car!
ADJECTIVE   VERB

Actor #2: You're worrying _____ .
ADVERB

Actor #1: Really? Look at the bellboy. He has my_____ in
NOUN

one hand, your _____ in the other, and his
NOUN

third hand...His *third* hand? Ahhhhh!

From GRAB BAG MAD LIBS® • Copyright © 2001, 1996 by Price Stern Sloan,
a division of Penguin Putnam Books for Young Readers, New York.

MAD LIBS® is fun to play with friends, but you can also play it by yourself! To begin with, DO NOT look at the story on the page below. Fill in the blanks on this page with the words called for. Then, using the words you have selected, fill in the blank spaces in the story.

Now you've created your own hilarious MAD LIBS® game!

IN THE GOOD OLD SUMMERTIME

PLURAL NOUN _____

PLURAL NOUN _____

ADVERB _____

VERB ENDING IN "ING" _____

ADJECTIVE _____

NUMBER _____

PART OF THE BODY _____

PLURAL NOUN _____

NOUN _____

PLURAL NOUN _____

TYPE OF LIQUID _____

NOUN _____

ADVERB _____

PLURAL NOUN _____

PLURAL NOUN _____

NOUN _____

NOUN _____

NOUN _____

NOUN _____

MAD☺LIBS®
IN THE GOOD
OLD SUMMERTIME

Many selective _____ prefer the Summer Olympics to
                      PLURAL NOUN

the Winter _____. They respond _____
            PLURAL NOUN   ADVERB

to such swimming and _____ competitions as the
                        VERB ENDING IN "ING"

hundred-meter _____-style race, the _____-meter
                ADJECTIVE   NUMBER

_____-stroke race, and, of course, the diving contests in
PART OF THE BODY

which _____ dive off a high _____ and do triple
        PLURAL NOUN   NOUN

_____ in the air before landing in the _____.
PLURAL NOUN   TYPE OF LIQUID

Equally fascinating are the track and _____ events in which
                                         NOUN

_____ conditioned _____ compete for gold
      ADVERB   PLURAL NOUN

_____. They compete in such exciting events as the 1,500-
PLURAL NOUN

_____ race, the hundred-_____ dash, the ever-
   NOUN   NOUN

popular _____ vaulting, and, last but not least, throwing
          NOUN

the hammer, the javelin, and the _____.
                                      NOUN

MAD LIBS® is fun to play with friends, but you can also play it by yourself! To begin with, DO NOT look at the story on the page below. Fill in the blanks on this page with the words called for. Then, using the words you have selected, fill in the blank spaces in the story.

Now you've created your own hilarious MAD LIBS® game!

GOOD MANNERS

NOUN _____

NOUN _____

NOUN _____

VERB _____

PART OF THE BODY _____

ADVERB_____

NOUN _____

NOUN _____

NOUN _____

NOUN _____

PART OF THE BODY (PLURAL) _____

NOUN _____

ADJECTIVE_____

ADVERB_____

MAD LIBS®
GOOD MANNERS

1. When you receive a birthday _____ or a wedding
   NOUN

   _____ , you should always send a thank-you
   NOUN

   _____ .
   NOUN

2. When you _____ or burp out loud, be sure to cover
   VERB

   your _____ and say, "I'm _____ sorry."
   PART OF THE BODY   ADVERB

3. If you are a man and wearing a/an _____ on your
   NOUN

   head and a/an _____ approaches, it's always
   NOUN

   polite to tip your _____ .
   NOUN

4. When you are at a friend's _____ for dinner,
   NOUN

   remember, it's not polite to eat with your _____ ,
   PART OF THE BODY (PLURAL)

   take food from anyone else's _____ , or leave the
   NOUN

   table before everyone else.

5. When meeting your friend's parents, always try to make a/an

   _____ impression by greeting them _____ .
   ADJECTIVE   ADVERB

MAD LIBS® is fun to play with friends, but you can also play it by yourself! To begin with, DO NOT look at the story on the page below. Fill in the blanks on this page with the words called for. Then, using the words you have selected, fill in the blank spaces in the story.

Now you've created your own hilarious MAD LIBS® game!

TV GUIDANCE
PICK OF THE WEEK

NOUN _____

ADJECTIVE _____

NUMBER _____

PLURAL NOUN _____

PLURAL NOUN _____

NOUN _____

PART OF THE BODY (PLURAL) _____

ADJECTIVE _____

PERSON IN ROOM (FEMALE) _____

NOUN _____

PART OF THE BODY _____

PLURAL NOUN _____

ADJECTIVE _____

ADJECTIVE _____

PERSON IN ROOM (FULL NAME) _____

NOUN _____

NOUN _____

MAD LIBS®
TV GUIDANCE
PICK OF THE WEEK

THURSDAY, 8:00 P.M. "My Adventures as a Foreign _____."
    NOUN

This is an exciting and _____ made-for-TV movie that
                ADJECTIVE

takes place during the time of World War _____. We give it
                        NUMBER

a rating of three _____.
        PLURAL NOUN

FRIDAY, 7:30 P.M. "Happy _____."
                PLURAL NOUN

When an old high-school _____ welcomes him with
                NOUN

open _____ and throws him a/an _____ party,
    PART OF THE BODY (PLURAL)   ADJECTIVE

this puts _____, his former _____
        PERSON IN ROOM (FEMALE)   NOUN

friend, into a bad state of _____.
                PART OF THE BODY

SATURDAY, 10:00 P.M. "Where Have All the _____ Gone?"
                        PLURAL NOUN

This _____ thriller, by the _____ director
        ADJECTIVE   ADJECTIVE

_____, is about a Manhattan _____
PERSON IN ROOM (FULL NAME)   NOUN

searching for a missing person in a small _____.
                        NOUN

From GRAB BAG MAD LIBS® • Copyright © 2001, 1996 by Price Stern Sloan,
a division of Penguin Putnam Books for Young Readers, New York.

MAD LIBS® is fun to play with friends, but you can also play it by yourself! To begin with, DO NOT look at the story on the page below. Fill in the blanks on this page with the words called for. Then, using the words you have selected, fill in the blank spaces in the story.

Now you've created your own hilarious MAD LIBS® game!

GOOD HEALTH TO ONE AND ALL

ADJECTIVE_____

ADJECTIVE_____

VERB ENDING IN "ING" _____

PART OF THE BODY (PLURAL) _____

PLURAL NOUN _____

PLURAL NOUN _____

NOUN _____

PLURAL NOUN _____

PLURAL NOUN _____

NOUN _____

PLURAL NOUN _____

PLURAL NOUN _____

ADJECTIVE_____

PLURAL NOUN _____

ADJECTIVE_____

ADJECTIVE_____

MAD LIBS®
GOOD HEALTH TO ONE AND ALL

A/an _____ fitness revolution is taking place. Today,
　　　　ADJECTIVE

millions of people are doing all kinds of _____ exercises
　　　　　　　　　　　　　　　　　　　ADJECTIVE

such as jogging, walking, and _____ to get their
　　　　　　　　　　　　VERB ENDING IN "ING"

_____ in shape and develop their _____.
PART OF THE BODY (PLURAL)　　　　　　　　　　　　PLURAL NOUN

Many go to gyms and health _____ to work out by
　　　　　　　　　　　PLURAL NOUN

punching a/an _____, lifting _____, or
　　　　　　NOUN　　　　　　　　　PLURAL NOUN

performing aerobic _____. In the past _____
　　　　　　　PLURAL NOUN　　　　　　　　　　NOUN

people have become very weight conscious. They have learned what

_____ they should and should not eat. They know it's
PLURAL NOUN

healthy to eat green _____ and _____ fruit.
　　　　　　　　PLURAL NOUN　　　　　ADJECTIVE

They also know to avoid foods high in _____ and
　　　　　　　　　　　　　　　　　PLURAL NOUN

_____ fats, especially if they want to lead a long and
ADJECTIVE

_____ life.
ADJECTIVE

MAD LIBS® is fun to play with friends, but you can also play it by yourself. To begin with, DO NOT look at the story on the page below. Fill in the blanks on this page with the words called for. Then, using the words you have selected, fill in the blank spaces in the story.

Now you've created your own hilarious MAD LIBS® game!

WHY DO SKUNKS SMELL?

NOUN _____

ADJECTIVE _____

PLURAL NOUN _____

PLACE _____

PLURAL NOUN _____

ADJECTIVE _____

NOUN _____

VERB ENDING IN "ING" _____

PART OF THE BODY _____

PART OF THE BODY (PLURAL) _____

PART OF THE BODY (PLURAL) _____

ADVERB _____

COLOR _____

PART OF THE BODY _____

PART OF THE BODY _____

WHY DO SKUNKS SMELL?

Surprisingly, a skunk is a friendly _____ who can
                                              NOUN

make a/an _____ household pet. But what makes these
                ADJECTIVE

_____ smell to high _____? The skunk has scent
   PLURAL NOUN   PLACE

_____ that contain a/an _____-smelling fluid.
   PLURAL NOUN   ADJECTIVE

When attacked, the skunk aims this smelly _____ at its enemies.
                                                   NOUN

But the skunk does give warning before _____. It
                                         VERB ENDING IN "ING"

raises its _____ first, or stamps its _____
            PART OF THE BODY   PART OF THE BODY (PLURAL)

so that you can run away as fast as your _____ can
                                          PART OF THE BODY (PLURAL)

carry you. The most _____ recognizable skunk is the
                        ADVERB

one with a _____ line on its _____ and
            COLOR   PART OF THE BODY

another one between its _____ and its ears.
                         PART OF THE BODY

From GRAB BAG MAD LIBS® • Copyright © 2001, 1996 by Price Stern Sloan,
a division of Penguin Putnam Books for Young Readers, New York.

MAD LIBS® is fun to play with friends, but you can also play it by yourself! To begin with, DO NOT look at the story on the page below. Fill in the blanks on this page with the words called for. Then, using the words you have selected, fill in the blank spaces in the story.

Now you've created your own hilarious MAD LIBS® game!

FAMOUS QUOTES FROM THE AMERICAN REVOLUTION

NOUN _____

NOUN _____

COLOR_____

PART OF THE BODY (PLURAL) _____

NOUN _____

PLURAL NOUN _____

VERB ENDING IN "ING" _____

NOUN _____

PLURAL NOUN _____

PLURAL NOUN _____

ADJECTIVE_____

NOUN_____

MAD LIBS®
FAMOUS QUOTES FROM
THE AMERICAN REVOLUTION

Nathan Hale said: "I regret that I have but one _____
                                                    NOUN

to give for my _____."
                      NOUN

William Prescott said: "Don't fire until you see the _____
                                                             COLOR

of their _____."
              PART OF THE BODY (PLURAL)

Patrick Henry said: "Give me liberty or give me _____."
                                                         NOUN

Paul Revere said: "The _____ are _____."
                             PLURAL NOUN   VERB ENDING IN "ING"

John Hancock said: "I wrote my _____ large so the king
                                        NOUN

could read it without his _____."
                                 PLURAL NOUN

Thomas Jefferson said: "All _____ are created equal. They
                                    PLURAL NOUN

are endowed by their creator with certain _____ rights
                                                    ADJECTIVE

and among these are life, liberty, and the pursuit of _____."
                                                               NOUN

This book is published by

PSS!

PRICE STERN SLOAN

whose other splendid titles include such literary classics as

The Original #1 Mad Libs®

Son of Mad Libs®

Sooper Dooper Mad Libs®

Monster Mad Libs®

Goofy Mad Libs®

Off-the-Wall Mad Libs®

Vacation Fun Mad Libs®

Camp Daze Mad Libs®

Christmas Fun Mad Libs®

Mad Libs® from Outer Space

Kid Libs®

Grab Bag Mad Libs®

Dinosaur Mad Libs®

Slam Dunk Mad Libs®

Night of the Living Mad Libs®

Upside-Down Mad Libs®

Mad Libs® 40th Anniversary Deluxe Edition

Mad Mad Mad Mad Mad Libs®

Mad Libs® On the Road

Mad Libs® In Love

Cool Mad Libs®

Haunted Mad Libs®

Prime-Time Mad Libs®

Straight "A" Mad Libs®

and many, many more!

Mad Libs® are available wherever books are sold.